Original title:
Echoes of Christmas Past

Copyright © 2024 Creative Arts Management OÜ
All rights reserved.

Author: Beckett Sinclair
ISBN HARDBACK: 978-9916-94-084-6
ISBN PAPERBACK: 978-9916-94-085-3

The Ghosts of Christmas Carols

In the attic, I found a song,
Two out of tune, and oh so wrong.
My cat joins in, with a meow so loud,
Creating a racket, feeling quite proud.

Neighbors peep in, their faces frown,
As I belt out tunes like a circus clown.
With jingles and jangles, I give it a try,
Even the ornaments seem to sigh.

Threads of Time and Tinsel

Remember the year we danced around?
With a tree that barely stood on the ground.
Tinsel tangled in our hair so bright,
We laughed till we cried, what a sight!

Grandma's cookies, a total flop,
Stuck to the pan, we gave them a mop.
But we gobbled them down, with giggles and glitz,
Who knew burnt sugar could taste like bliss?

Warmth of Hot Cocoa Remains

The mugs are chipped, yet still we sip,
Cocoa spills as the marshmallows slip.
Frothy mustaches and giggling glee,
It's a chocolatey war zone, just wait and see!

Mom says to stir, but we just dive,
Flavors collide, oh how we thrive!
Sipping and slurping, causing a scene,
Hot cocoa battles are fit for a queen!

Songs of Seasons Gone By

On the record player, the tunes play loud,
A mix of giggles, a wobbly crowd.
Each note brings back a silly dance,
As we twirl and stumble, lost in a trance.

The jingle bell moments, now worn and frayed,
Make us chuckle, in memories swayed.
With every chorus, a story unfolds,
Of laughter and mischief, tales to be told.

Silk Ribbons and Wrapped Hearts

In a closet, gifts lie tight,
Tangled ribbons of red and white.
Squeaky toys from years gone by,
My cat thinks they're hers to try.

Grandma's knitting, oh what a sight,
Hats made for dogs, oh what a fright!
Laughter echoes through the hall,
As Uncle Joe wears one so small.

Connecting Threads of Generations

Old photos show us silly hats,
Worn by cousins, liked by rats.
Sledding down the hill in pairs,
Who knew snow was filled with glares?

Auntie's fruitcake, dense and bold,
It could probably fend off cold.
Each bite met with laughter and cheer,
Why do we make this every year?

Frosted Breath and Warm Spirits

Frosted breath like puffs of steam,
Snowman's nose? A carrot dream.
Hot cocoa spills on my old coat,
Just one more sip, I'll surely float!

Caroling with dogs in tow,
Barking loud in chilly glow.
Neighbors peek from windows wide,
As we trip down the snowy slide.

Joy Wrapped in Yesterday's Warmth

Wrapping paper strewn about,
Like confetti from a shout.
Rowdy kids and silly games,
Who knew joy comes with such claims?

Grandpa cracks his jokes with flair,
Using puns that fill the air.
We roll with laughter, can't hold back,
Each silly tale keeps us on track.

Traces of Evening Light

The twinkling lights reflect our cheer,
They blink like tipsy folks at the bar.
Grandma's fruitcake, we all hold dear,
Yet it lands like a meteor from afar.

Mittens lost in a heated chase,
A cat wrestles with ribbon and bows.
Snowflakes dance with a silly grace,
While we try to avoid the hot cocoa flows.

Cradles of Holiday Dreams

Visions of sugarplums sweep through the night,
Yet all I see are leftovers on plates.
The cookies vanished - what a delight!
Did Santa come, or just grab some crates?

Mom's idea of 'just a sprig' is a tree,
With ornaments perched like they're on a ride.
When the dog jumps, it's pure jubilee,
A holiday wonderland turned wild slide.

The Spirit of December's Glow

The carolers sing off-key with glee,
A reindeer costume almost fits.
Each note a shout, 'come sing with me!'
Even if our voices are a bit hits and bits.

Wrapping gifts in paper like a scene,
It unravels during the grand reveal.
"Did you want a toy or a pastel marine?"
Oh, the joy when surprise turns real!

Tales Woven in Evergreen

Storytime by the crackling fire,
Dad's tales get taller each year, it seems.
He claims the tree once aimed for higher,
Yet its height is the stuff of our dreams.

As we sip cider with laughter and fun,
The dog steals the last piece of pie.
Yet, grumbling, we cherish the run,
In this holiday mix-up, we all comply.

Faded Photographs in Time

Old laughs caught in yellowed frames,
Smiles like ornaments, playing silly games.
A cat in a hat, what a sight to see,
Whiskers in the tinsel, where's the catnip tree?

Uncle Joe's sweater, a sight to behold,
Knitted by grandma, warm but so bold.
A mustache of snowflakes, his look was a hoot,
By the fireplace he'd dance, in mismatched suit.

Starlit Tales of the Elders

Grandpa tells stories, a twinkle in eyes,
Of reindeer on rooftops, and Christmas surprise.
A sleigh ride to nowhere, just boredom and cheer,
With snow in his beard, who'd have thought he'd steer?

Aunt Mary's fruitcake, a brick if you please,
Used once as a doorstop, now propped with ease.
"Just a slice!" she insists, with a wink and a smile,
While we plot our escape to the bathroom, in style.

Bathing in Candle Glow

Glow from the candles, a flicker delight,
But somehow, Aunt Edna, has lost her sight.
She's wearing the wreath, round her neck like a shawl,
"Just adding some flair!" she proclaims to us all.

The cookies all burned, a charcoal surprise,
We joke as we nibble, oh how time flies!
With milk spilled on carpet, a laugh we won't lack,
As Elf on the Shelf lays flat on his back.

Hushed Conversations Under the Bough

Whispers of children, secrets and giggles,
Under the tree, as the low light wiggles.
"Is Santa real, or just a big jest?"
Mom rolls her eyes, "Well, what do you expect?"

A forgotten gift, lost in the fray,
An empty box wrapped, it sits in dismay.
"Surprise!" we all cheer, till we figure it out,
Now it's a treasure hunt—of that there's no doubt.

The Magic within Winter's Embrace

Snowflakes dance on rooftops high,
Every child lets out a sigh.
The dog in boots, a clumsy sight,
Chases shadows in pure delight.

Hot cocoa spills while laughter reigns,
A snowman's hat, too big, it claims.
Sleds go flying, a wild ride,
With giggles lost in winter's tide.

Grandma's tales of Christmas cheer,
Get funnier with every beer.
An ailing bird that flew away,
Brought laughter to our joyful day.

In every corner, mischief calls,
With tinsel stuck on window halls.
The magic here, so sheer and bright,
Keeps us warm through this frosty night.

When Wishes Become Memories

A pickle hunt in a tree so tall,
Unwrap the laughter, let it sprawl.
The gifts that bounced and rolled away,
Turn memory lanes to bright ballet.

Cookies burnt, the kitchen's war,
The dog is sneaking by the door.
The cat steals ribbons, adds to the fun,
As we all shout, "Let's not tell mom!"

Wish lists written with crayons bold,
Wishes once made, now tales retold.
The magic of youth, it slips, it bends,
With every laugh, and pranks of friends.

When night falls down, the stars arise,
With spiced eggnog and silly ties.
Mom's face lit by the twinkling light,
Holds memories where our hearts take flight.

Lanterns through the Winter's Veil

Lanterns flicker, shadows play,
As frosty breath turns night to day.
The snowman winks, it's quite absurd,
His carrot nose, a little blurred.

Jingle bells and pots that hop,
The cat gets stuck in a gift shop.
With mittens lost and scarves all tangled,
We stumble forth, with giggles wrangled.

The tree stands tall with quirks galore,
Tangled lights and a squirrel's roar.
With each mishap a laugh will bloom,
It lights up even the dullest room.

So here we stand, in frosty cheer,
With tales of joy that draw us near.
In winter's grip, the warmth we find,
Are memories built in love entwined.

Garlands of Long-Lost Smiles

In the attic, sweaters so bright,
A reindeer design, what a sight!
A knitted treasure, quite a crime,
We wore it proudly, oh so prime.

Grandma's cookies, slightly charred,
They crumbled like dreams, it was hard.
We laughed and choked, 'Is that a nut?'
Or did we taste the garden's glut?

Old photos with silly grins,
Faded memories where fun begins.
The tree was lopsided, oh what fun,
And every gift? A sock, not one!

With garlands strung, and hearts so light,
The laughter found in winter's night.
Oh, the tales from those silly days,
Are treasures wrapped in love's warm blaze.

Flickering Stories from the Attic

Up in the attic, boxes galore,
Dusty old tales we can't ignore.
A toy soldier, missing an arm,
He still stands guard, he's got the charm.

Tinsel tangled, what a mess,
Each strand a story, we confess.
Mom's old elf, with a crooked grin,
A dubious smile, let the fun begin!

The tree fell down, what a scene,
Cats claimed victory, oh so mean!
Yet still we dance, to the old tunes,
While laughs and light fill up the rooms.

With candles glowing, we recall,
The silly tricks that made us fall.
Each flicker brings a chuckle forth,
As warmth and wit remind our worth.

Candlelight Chronicles

Candles flicker, shadows play,
Old tales emerge in their ballet.
Dad's bad jokes, we roll our eyes,
Yet laugh until the tears arise.

The mistletoe, a strategic ploy,
Caused more chaos than joy.
We duck and dodge as family sways,
In this odd dance, love always stays.

Gifts misplaced, they caused a feud,
And Auntie sighed, 'What's the mood?'
But laughter wins, it fills the air,
As we tease each other without care.

Candlelight reveals our truths,
And warms the heart like childhood's youth.
With stories told and smiles anew,
We find the joy in silly do's.

Harmony of Old Christmas Songs

A harmony rings from the past,
With tunes that dance, oh so fast.
Granddad sings off-key, oh dear,
Yet we all cheer, and hold him near.

Jingle bells, but someone tripped,
Over the dog and promptly flipped.
With laughter echoing through the hall,
We share our joy, we never fall.

Hot cocoa spills from tiny hands,
A marshmallow fight, 'Don't make demands!'
We giggle and dash, oh what a treat,
As songs blend with stomping feet.

Old carols sung with flair and zest,
Mom's twist makes us all jest.
In this chorus, there's bliss to share,
For laughter rings through winter's air.

Frosted Dreams of Yore

Snowflakes drift like ancient ghosts,
Creating scenes we love the most.
The kitchen smells of burnt fruitcake,
A holiday thrill we won't forsake.

Cats in sweaters, oh what a sight,
Pouncing softly in the silent night.
Grandpa's snoring, a loud refrain,
While tales of elves twist in his brain.

Bright lights twinkle, a tree gone wild,
Beneath it, chaos of a joyful child.
Future pets might wear a hat,
Oh, the joys of a tangled cat!

And though the years keep marching on,
These frosted dreams are never gone.
We'll laugh till we ache, then doze off fast,
In this jolly realm of memories past.

Soft Laughter Beneath the Mistletoe

Underneath where mischief thrives,
Silly kids plotting wild high-fives.
A secret kiss, a face gone red,
As mistletoe hangs, dreams are fed.

Uncle's beard is way too long,
He starts to sing a silly song.
A partridge in a pear tree steals the show,
While clumsy cousins trip in snow.

Hot cocoa spills on grandma's lap,
With giggles and a happy clap.
Dance moves that make us all glare,
But who could care with joy to share?

Laughter rings through frosty night,
A lovely mix of cheer and fright.
These moments, stitched in every heart,
Beneath the mistletoe, we play our part.

Nostalgic Caroling Melodies

Caroling round the block so bright,
With off-key tunes in the chilly night.
Neighbors peek from curtains drawn,
As we bellow 'til the break of dawn.

Potholes hidden under heaps of snow,
Watch our singers sadly go slow.
The dog joins in with a barking cheer,
Creating sounds that only we hear.

Candles flicker with a soft, warm glow,
While voices clash, it's quite the show.
Who knew that singing could bring such glee,
When the only notes belong to me?

Oh, the nostalgia warms the air,
As we sing loud, without a care.
For every note we sing off-key,
Holds a memory — pure and free.

Silent Footsteps on Winter's Path

Crunching snow beneath our feet,
Playing tag in the winter's heat.
Snowmen grin with carrot noses,
While laughter bursts like blooming roses.

Our playful fight with snowball flares,
Each missile thrown with crazy glares.
Until a grandpa slips on ice,
His comedic flair is quite precise.

Mom's socks wrapped on our frozen toes,
Thanks to warmth from winter's prose.
We trace our paths in patterns odd,
Each footfall plays a leading cod.

As shadows lengthen, the day is done,
We'll walk back home, our hearts have fun.
With giggles fading into the night,
These footsteps shine with pure delight.

Snowflakes Dancing in Dusk

Snowflakes twirl with glee,
A dance in the chilly air.
Old folks slip and shout,
"Where's that darn walking chair?"

Hot cocoa spills with grace,
Marshmallows on the floor.
Grandma's secret recipe,
Turns the kitchen into a war!

The cat leaps, the tree shakes,
Ornaments start to slide.
"I swear that squirrel's been here,"
As we all giggle and hide.

Laughter fills the night sky,
With sprinkles of merry cheer.
Forgetful Uncle Bob trips,
And we all toast with a cheer!

When Time Pauses for a Moment

Snowmen watch with wide eyes,
As kids play a wild game.
A selfie stick in hand,
Uncle Joe's the main claim to fame.

The roast chicken took a dive,
Right onto Aunt Sue's shoe.
"It's just a little baste,"
She laughs, "No doubt this will brew!"

The old record spins again,
Why is it stuck on replay?
With every scratch and skip,
We dance in a funky way!

Time slows as we all feast,
Silly jokes fill the air.
'Till Dad falls asleep mid-bite,
With turkey dreams for a chair!

Lullabies of the Winter Solstice

Under the twinkling lights,
We gather round so bright.
A cat naps on the gifts,
While dogs steal all the bites.

The carols are off-key,
As we all try to sing,
Grandpa's snoring with joy,
As we search for the ring.

Cookies hidden too well,
Fall into secret hands.
"Who ate all the crescents?"
The dog just sits and stands.

With bells and glow sticks out,
We cheer as night goes on.
Tomorrow's woes forgotten,
'Til the new year comes along!

Invitations to the Past's Embrace

Old photos come to life,
With hairstyles bold and proud.
Aunt Beth in a snowstorm,
Her laugh is still so loud.

Kids swing from candy canes,
While grandpa fixes lights.
"Whose turn to hang the star?"
Oh, those holiday fights!

Mismatched socks with flair,
Show off stories yet untold.
"Do you remember last year?"
As memories unfold.

The night is filled with warmth,
With silly stunts and games.
Invitations to join in,
Is how love always claims!

Peeking Through Shuttered Windows

Children giggle behind closed eyes,
Peeking through the festive ties.
Snowflakes tickle their bright pink noses,
Laughter spills as joy overflows.

Grandpa's beard, a snowy fright,
Chasing kids who dart in fright.
Santa's belly on a thrill ride,
Whiskers jingle but no one hides.

Cookies crumble, milk's a must,
Mice plot mischief, in cheese we trust.
Gifts stacked high with ribbons tossed,
All while cat claims the box, so bossed!

Through each prank, a memory stays,
The fun, the laughter, in silly plays.
Even when the door's tightly shut,
The holiday spirit won't let up!

Heartstrings Tied in Red

Ribbons twist like tangled twine,
Tinsel battles with the pine.
A caroler singing with a twist,
Forget the lyrics? No one's missed!

Aunt Betty's wigs, a jarring sight,
Party hats that just don't fit right.
Goofy sweaters, grandpa grins,
The dancing starts and the laughter wins!

Every gift bears a funny tag,
Last year's fruitcake in a ragged bag.
Family stories, snorts and sighs,
Watch as Uncle Jerry tries to fly!

Love's wrapped tight in mismatched bows,
Each season's charm dramatically shows.
With heartstrings tugged and smiles so fair,
In laughter, we find the best care!

Cool Night Air, Warm Hearts

Under stars with frosty breath,
Snowmen dance, defying death.
Children chatter, tiny shoes,
Sleds go whizzing with bright hues.

Hot cocoa spills on grandma's lap,
"Just one more marshmallow!"—a trap!
Laughter bubbles, joy takes flight,
Frostbite tales nearly ignite!

Mittens lost in the snowy drift,
Finding them brings a sweet gift.
Dad's dance moves, a sight to behold,
Looks like Rudolph's gone directly cold!

So we gather, spirits aglow,
In the chill, our love will grow.
For warmth comes from laughter shared,
In every tale, it's love declared!

Unraveled Threads of Tradition

Old ornaments, stories to tell,
On crooked branches, they do dwell.
Lights blink twice in a quirky sync,
Grandma's wink just made you think!

The fruitcake? It's still around,
A relic from the past profound.
Socks mismatched, nobody cares,
Crafting joy in humble flares.

In the kitchen, flour fights,
Rolling dough through festive nights.
Mom's big hat is quite the sight,
Watch out! She's armed with a spatula fight!

Each year repeats the funny lore,
With giggles echoing from every door.
Though time may twist and threads may fray,
Our laughter binds us, come what may!

Remnants of Joyful Mirth

Old sweaters dug from bins,
With patterns wild and free,
A tree of mismatched decor,
Bringing joy and glee.

Leftover fruitcake in a box,
A weight-lifting feat,
It's gifted once again to friends,
A holiday repeat!

Ugly sweaters worn with pride,
In pictures full of cheer,
Each year they come and bring out laughs,
As memories draw near.

Socks that never find their mate,
A mystery each year,
We joke about their daring flight,
As laughter fills the sphere.

Reflections in Candlelight

Candles flicker, shadows dance,
On faces full of cheer,
Grandma's recipe burns just right,
And fills the air with beer?

Tinsel stuck in Dad's beard,
An angel on the shelf,
"You can't wear that to dinner!"
"It's just my festive self!"

The gift that never was to be,
Regifted once again,
It's wrapped in paper from last year,
And marked a "Dear old friend."

A cat that climbs the Christmas tree,
And thinks it's all a game,
As ornaments come crashing down,
The holiday's to blame!

Footprints in the Snow

Footprints lead to nowhere fast,
In snow that's soft and bright,
Was that a deer or Uncle Joe?
Who wore shoes way too tight?

Snowmen built with silly hats,
With carrots as their nose,
They stand watch o'er our antics,
As winter laughter flows.

Sleds that launched us down the hill,
With screams that filled the air,
We tumbled through the frosty breeze,
And giggled without care.

Yet in the end, we warmed our toes,
By fireside tales untold,
With cocoa mugs and stories shared,
A winter's night of gold.

Echoing Laughter Under the Stars

Beneath a sky that's sprinkled bright,
With laughter in the air,
We share the tales of yesteryear,
In pajamas that we wear.

The reindeer games we used to play,
At Grandma's cheer-filled home,
And Auntie's dance that made us laugh,
While Dad just stared and groaned.

Silly hats and jingle bells,
Our chorus off the chart,
It's off-key yet full of mirth,
A symphony of heart.

As stars twinkle and night grows old,
These moments shine so bright,
With laughter shared and stories told,
We savor pure delight.

Through the Eyes of a Child

Snowflakes dance in swirling flight,
A jolly laugh, pure delight.
Stockings stuffed with mismatched toys,
Oh, the joy that fills our boys.

Cookies left for Santa's team,
They sneak and nibble, pure ice cream.
Whispers soft, a secret shared,
In dreams of magic, none compared.

The tree's a giant made of light,
With tinsel glistening, oh what a sight!
Imagined sleigh bells through the night,
Each magic hour, a new delight.

Wrap them tight in giant bows,
Squeals of laughter as the chaos grows.
The world is big, and oh so bright,
Through youthful eyes, it feels just right.

Rustic Snowmen in Ghostly Gardens

Snowmen stand with crooked grins,
A hat too big, a scarf with spins.
Button eyes that somewhat sway,
They plot new tricks on winter's day.

In the garden, ghosts of cheer,
Whisper tales we cannot hear.
Twinkling lights in every tree,
Waving warmly, come and see!

A carrot nose that sneezes snow,
A wink and nod, 'I stole the show!'
They're plotting mischief, can't you tell?
These frosty friends, they cast a spell.

Hot cocoa brewing, marshmallows fly,
Snowflakes laugh as they drift by.
Rustic fun, we can't ignore,
With snowmen dancing, who could ask for more?

The Sweet Aroma of Cinnamon

Cinnamon sticks tucked in a jar,
A scent that travels, near and far.
Laughter bubbles like boiling stew,
Sweetened treats for me and you.

Grandma's hands, a sprinkle here,
Doughnuts rising, oh what a cheer!
Cookies stacked in towers so tall,
Hide a few, but not for all!

Frosty windows, patterns drawn,
The smell of spice greets the dawn.
Baking battles, flour fights,
Misadventures, oh such delights!

Warmth and giggles fill the air,
Who knew butter could dance and flare?
In every bite, a cozy tale,
Flavors swirl like a snowy gale!

Carved Wooden Memories

Wooden toys with tales to tell,
A puppet's grin, he rides so well.
Trains that chug and dolls that dance,
Each crafted piece holds a chance.

Whittled laughs from grandpa's hands,
Sailing ships made from soft pine strands.
Every scratch is love, it's true,
Each tiny flaw adds charm anew.

Worn-out blocks of color bright,
Stacked so high, they reach new height.
Imagined lands on bedroom floors,
Unlocking dreams behind closed doors.

Time can't fade these treasured toys,
Infused with smiles and childhood joys.
Carved with laughter, love, and care,
Each wooden memory, shining rare.

Lanterns of Memory's Glow.

In the attic, toys all stacked,
A Santa lost a boot, that's whacked!
Old garlands tangled like a web,
A cat's new throne, quite the celeb.

Cookies baked that looked like slugs,
Nana swore they had no bugs!
With cocoa spilled on Grandma's dress,
We laughed so hard, we felt the stress.

Dad dressed up, a sight so funny,
Looked like something from a punny!
A reindeer hat awry, askew,
And laughter ringing, bright and true.

So raise a toast to silly days,
With lanterns shining in folly's blaze!
For memories dance with every grin,
In cheer and chuckles, let's begin!

Whispers of Yuletide Memories

In a snowy scene, we slipped and slid,
Head first into a pile, oh, what a bid!
The snowman lost its carrot nose,
We laughed so hard, who really knows?

Grandpa's jokes, so cheesy and bold,
Told every year, oh, they never get old!
The dog stole cookies while we all cheered,
A festive heist, how we all jeered.

Lights that flicker, some are quite dim,
While Uncle Bob starts to sing on a whim!
Off-key notes in the chilly air,
Joy found in laughter, too much to bear.

So share the tales of mishaps past,
In the warmth of love, we hold steadfast!
With each silly story told today,
We pave a path in our own funny way!

Shadows of Frosty Mornings

Woke up to frost, a dazzling sight,
But socks mismatched, oh, what a fright!
The snowball fight began with flair,
While Dad got hit, his shocked despair!

Hot cocoa spilled, a splash on the floor,
Mom's frowning face, we all want more!
Dancing on ice, what a grand show,
Until we fell, oh, how we'd glow!

The cat in the tree, a festive plight,
As ornaments flew in a wild flight!
Yet still we cheer, with all our might,
In shadows of laughter, hearts feel light.

So gather 'round, with giggles loud,
In the frosty morning, we feel so proud!
For years will come, we'll smile and share,
The funny tales that hung in the air!

Remnants of Twinkling Lights

The lights are up, but one's gone dead,
A jingle bell's stuck in the dog's head!
Mama's falling while she tries to dance,
In mismatched socks, she takes a chance.

Grandpa's glasses, they sit on his nose,
With ribbons tangled, in hilarious rows!
The turkey's burnt, a charred delight,
While all the kids await their bite.

The mistletoe hangs, a sticky trap,
Where Uncle Joe took a silly nap!
Caught under there, a cheeky smack,
"Oh joy!" he shouts, "I'll take that back!"

So let the lights twinkle with cheer,
As each silly moment we hold dear!
In laughter's glow, we find the light,
In remnants of joy, all feels right!

Almanacs of Frost and Cheer

In a corner, old socks sit,
Holding treasures, all quite a bit.
With candy canes in every fold,
And stories waiting to be retold.

Grandma's fruitcake, tough as a shoe,
Sits in the pantry, a mystery stew.
We dare each other to take a slice,
"A delicacy!" we'd think twice.

Wreaths that looked like rolled-up grass,
Hoping to find a long-lost class.
They giggle at how it used to shine,
Now just a reminder of hay and twine.

Snowmen grinning, noses askew,
Wonder if they were ever true.
With carrot noses and floppy hats,
They sway and sigh, "How about that?"

Echoing Laughter Across the Ages

A jolly ghost with a wink in his eyes,
Lists last year's blunders, oh, how time flies!
Spilling eggnog on Uncle Joe's shoe,
Turning the party into a zoo.

The cat with tinsel, a festive mess,
Wore the decorations with pure finesse.
He climbed the tree, oh, what a sight!
And gave the ornaments a wild flight!

The holiday cards, a crown of cheer,
Barely remembered from last year!
A photo where dad wore a green wig,
Not quite the memory one would dig.

As midnight chimes, the jokes resume,
"Who stole the cookies?" fills the room.
With laughter ringing through the night,
An endless cycle, pure delight!

Underneath the Boughs of Memory

Beneath the tree, a dustball spree,
Old toys whisper tales, just wait and see.
Rudolph's nose, a bulb gone stale,
Once sparkled bright, now tells a tale.

In the attic, a rusty sleigh,
Holds secrets of games from yesterday.
Once powered by voices, bright and loud,
Now it serves as a dusty shroud.

A mouse parade beneath the lights,
Nibbling crumbs of festive nights.
They dance on cookie crumbs galore,
Creating a ruckus we can't ignore!

Yet another gift wrapped up in glee,
A mixtape lost in the history.
Each song a chuckle, some cringe with fright,
"Who made this?" echoes through the night!

Tread Softly on Yesteryear's Snow

Upon the porch, the boots still lie,
Muffled laughter, a snowball's fly.
Granddad slips with a comedic flair,
As snowflakes frolic without a care.

Pictures in frames, with faces that glow,
Look closer—did your aunt steal the show?
Dressed as an elf, with shoes too tight,
Her face is priceless, what a delight!

Christmas lights tangled in old cords,
A battle for space with scissors and boards.
Some lights flicker with rebellious pride,
While others remind us of joy that's inside.

So here we are, with laughter in tow,
Recalling moments that chime with a glow.
Under the stars, the laughs ring true,
In the warmth of family, we renew!

Ghosts of Snowball Fights

Huddled near the frosty tree,
We aimed with glee, not a thought to flee.
Lumps of snow took flight on cue,
Laughter rang as we all flew.

But one missed shot went astray,
Hit Aunt Mabel, what a display!
She raised her arms in shock and despair,
Then joined us with snow in her hair.

A snowman formed by the bitter fight,
Squished and rounded, a comical sight.
With carrot nose slightly askew,
Who knew snow could hold such a brew?

As memories melt in the warmth, we cheer,
Recalling the fights that brought us near.
Though snow now melts with a soft sigh,
The ghost of laughter will never die.

Evergreens Whispering Old Secrets

Beneath the tree, a whisper spent,
Those needles hold tales of merriment.
When grandpa danced with a twinkle in eye,
Wobbling around, made us all sigh.

Each ornament tells its own strange tale,
Missed the hook and then went stale.
A ceramic cat with a lopsided grin,
Once fell, caused chaos, we let the fun begin.

They've seen the feasts and the family fun,
Socks on the floor, a wild run.
That squirrel with a penchant for cheer,
Tried to steal treats but disappeared.

With each branch, secrets unfurl,
Tinsel glimmers in a laugh-filled whirl.
These evergreens know how to make jest,
A reminder of love and a warm, silly quest.

The Embrace of Homemade Treats

In the kitchen, chaos abounds,
Flour clouds like snowy mounds.
A whisk takes flight in a jubilant twirl,
Mom lands in dough, oh what a whirl!

Cookies shaped like reindeer and stars,
Tasting the dough, oh, the bizarre!
Just a pinch of love and a dash of cheer,
Dropping sprinkles, it's festive in here.

Burnt batches went flying from the pan,
"Not my fault!" cried the maker of the clan.
Yet piles of goodies made all things bright,
Sweets in the air on that merry night.

With laughter and crumbs strewn about,
The kitchen felt like a giggly shout.
Even burnt treats with bits of glee,
Warmed hearts more than the best cup of tea.

Trinkets from Times Gone By

Dusty boxes hide treasures galore,
Old toys and trinkets, who could ask for more?
A teddy bear with a battered seam,
Whispers of playtime, a sweet childhood dream.

Grandma's brooch with a missing stone,
Tells tales of when she wasn't alone.
A faded postcard from a far-off shore,
Invites us to laugh, to smile, and explore.

That pesky clock with its stubborn tick,
Never quite worked, but it surely did trick!
It chimed loudly at the silliest hour,
Bringing laughter like a bright wildflower.

Each trinket's a giggle, a whisper of days,
Full of mischief, a charming craze.
With each find, we celebrate the past,
In laughter and joy, the moments forever last.

Visions of Winter's Embrace

Snowflakes dance with glee,
As we fumble with our tea.
The cat's in the tree, oh what a sight,
Unruly furball in festive delight.

Socks mismatched, a true delight,
Uncle Joe yells, "Not too tight!"
Reindeer games get out of hand,
With snowballs flying, we make our stand.

Grandma's fruitcake, still not gone,
We share a laugh; it's still quite strong.
Tinsel tangled, it's a mess,
But we all agree—hey, who could guess?

Mugs of cocoa overflow,
As stories bounce to and fro.
Each laugh, a spark, each tale, a blast,
In a winter's hug, we've found our cast.

Flurries of Memory

Fluffy snow in every nook,
Who needs a recipe book?
A snowman with a crooked grin,
Wears last year's scarf, it's a win.

Mom's cooking fills the air,
But she forgot the pie, beware!
A burnt batch turned crisp and black,
Still, we laugh, and dine off track.

Auntie's stories come alive,
With twinkling eyes, we all dive.
Her dance moves? A dreadful sight,
But we cheer her on with sheer delight.

Carols sung at the top of our lungs,
While Dad dances, we're all young.
In this chaos, joy is cast,
In the warm embrace of a joyous past.

A Glance at the Glittering Past

Ornaments hang, a bit askew,
Each one tells a tale, it's true.
A photo with a cat on display,
Napping 'neath branches, it stole the day.

A gift that squeaks, what a surprise,
Even the dog can't hide his eyes.
Tangled lights, a homeowners' bane,
Yet we plug them in and smile through the pain.

Cookies made but burnt to bits,
Taste testers? Everyone sits.
With every bite, we share a cheer,
Embracing the chaos, year after year.

Grandpa's jokes, the same old lines,
Still they hit, like vintage wines.
In glimmering nights with smiles amassed,
We find pure joy in the contrasts.

The Enchantment of Familiar Faces

Gather 'round the table, a jovial sight,
With laughter and stories that feel just right.
The pie that's lopsided, with a wink and a cheer,
We claim it's tradition, pulling closer near.

The lights flicker, as adults debate,
Who fell asleep first, it's never too late.
And Uncle Bob, with his tales of yore,
Keeps us wondering if there's more in store.

Mismatched sweaters, a fashion show,
Will these trends come back? Way to go!
Each silly snap, a treasure to keep,
As we laugh like children, awake from the deep.

A toast to the chaos, both silly and grand,
With joy that remains, no matter the plan.
Through all the fun and slightly askew,
We find in these moments, our history true.

Whispers of Yule Long Gone

In the attic lies an old, wrinkled hat,
Santa wore it, or was it the cat?
Dust bunnies dance to a ho-ho tune,
While old stockings droop like a wounded balloon.

The cookies we baked turned out like bricks,
Made a fine doorstop between the pricks.
Our tree leaned sideways, a fragile sight,
As we laughed and cheered, 'It's a festive plight!'

Grandma's baked ham was a mystery meat,
A prize for the bravest, a culinary feat.
We chewed and grimaced, just trying to smile,
As visions of dinners made the night worthwhile.

So raise a toast to the quirky and sweet,
In memories wrapped warm, a laugh's our treat.
May your holidays spark joy, not dread,
With hats and mishaps, and laughter instead!

Memories Wrapped in Tinsel

The carols we sang were off-key and bold,
Like cats in a blender, a sight to behold.
Yet Grandma would smile, with her twinkling cheer,
"At least it's not silent, let's keep it near!"

Our lights flickered bright, a electrical thrill,
Until one shorted out, gave Dad quite a chill.
He jumped like a squirrel, then shouted with glee,
"At least now there's ambiance; let it be free!"

The gifts were amusing, socks all in a row,
Shaped like a pickle, or a fuzzy bow.
We'd giggle and laugh, unwrapping the jest,
Finding joy in the silly, that was our best.

So let's raise our mugs full of spiced cider,
To moments of laughter that couldn't grow wider.
For wrapped in our laughter, each memory glows,
As through all these tales, our happiness flows!

Shadows of the Frosted Hearth

Sipping cocoa from mugs, chipped and stained,
With marshmallows floating like snowmen untrained.
The fire crackles softly, with shadows that leap,
While we recall stories that make our hearts weep.

The cat stole the turkey, we chased in a fright,
Slipping on reruns of '90s delights.
The chaos of family, the warmth and the tears,
Around the frosted hearth, we faced all our fears.

Bright paper flowered all through the house,
Until Frida the squirrel brought down the spouse.
He scattered the tinsel in jolly despair,
Leaving us chuckling, with glee in the air.

Comedies played on repeat through the night,
With laughter contagious, oh what pure delight!
So gather 'round friends, with cheer and good cheer,
For moments like these will ever endear!

Gleams of a Winter's Eve

The snowflakes danced in shapes quite absurd,
Like penguins on ice, each flap was unheard.
As we bundled up tight, our noses turned red,
We ventured outside, while the hot cocoa fled.

The sleds went flying, but mainly off track,
With bodies in piles, that's how we came back.
The laughter erupted with every bright crash,
As winter's sweet madness brought forth a quick splash.

We built a snowman, who toppled with flair,
Sporting Dad's scarf, and a lost teddy bear.
Eyes made of coal, and a hat out of dog,
The joy turned to silly; that's what we log!

So here's to the shine of those evenings aglow,
To giggles and snowdrifts, the fun that they sow.
May each winter's eve sparkle with joy, a must,
With friends by our side, in laughter we trust!

Lost Time Beneath the Stars

The stars are out, quite merry and bright,
But where's my gift? It's vanished from sight!
I checked the fridge, I checked the shoe,
Turns out, it was in my pocket. Who knew?

The tree's decked out with tinsel and cheer,
Yet the cat decided it would be a deer.
He pounced and rolled, with shiny delight,
Leaving us laughing 'til well past midnight.

Grandma's fruitcake, a mystery indeed,
Unwrapped, it bounced; it seemed to have speed!
We tossed it around like a festive ball,
And cheered as it took a grand leap and fall.

With glasses raised, we toast to the night,
A comedy show wrapped in fables bright.
Each laugh a star, twinkling above,
Remembering moments we dearly love.

Of Angels and Winter Whimsy

The snowflakes dance, but my nose is red,
I slipped on ice, but I'll just blame Fred.
He promised the path was clear, oh dear!
Now I'm doing circles, with much winter cheer.

Angels on tree tops, so perfectly placed,
But my nephew took one, it's a wild chase!
He giggles and runs, high on holiday sweets,
While we're stuck with tinsel stuck to our feets.

Hot cocoa flows like a river of bliss,
But someone added chili, what a hit-or-miss.
"It's festive!" I said, with a grin on my face,
As my taste buds danced in a spicy embrace.

With carols sung in a slightly wrong key,
We harmonize chaos, oh what a decree!
The warmth of our laughter fills up the whole room,
And out of the chaos, new memories bloom.

Hallowed Hallways of Twinkling Joy

The hallways are lined with old, flickering lights,
  While Dad tells the story of his crazy flights.
  He claimed he once flew up high like a kite,
But Mom just rolled her eyes—Oh, what a sight!

Stockings hung low, with treats and some socks,
  But let's not discuss how many we've lost.
  The dog found a candy that spilled on the rug,
Now he prances around, his tail like a bug.

Mistletoe hangs, yet no kiss will be had,
'Cause Uncle Joe's here, acting all kinds of bad.
He'll dance like a chicken to make us all laugh,
  As we battle with giggles, trying to staff!

In hallowed halls, where laughter rings true,
  Memories linger, like the taste of fondue.
  We're making new tales, with each little jest,
In the heart of our home, where love knows no rest.

An Old Familiar Song Resounds

An old tune plays, but the words slip my mind,
As Sis starts to croon, a mix-up so blind.
"Jingle Bells" melds with some rap in a twist,
And we laugh 'til our sides ache—now isn't that bliss?

Grandpa's at piano, all fingers and toes,
He sings o'er the keys, a melody flows.
But oops! There's a cat, and he leaps with delight,
Straight onto the keys, oh what a sight!

With cookies in hand and icing galore,
We try to bake goodies, but who needs a score?
The dough's a disaster, but spirits are high,
We munch on the crumbs as we let laughter fly.

So here's to the sounds that make our hearts sing,
To the quirks of the season, oh what joy they bring!
Each note's a reminder, a chuckle, a call,
That love wrapped in laughter is the best gift of all.

Slumbering Secrets of the Season

In the attic, the tree lies low,
With lights like stars and a jolly glow.
Forgotten tinsel, a cat on the stair,
Whispering tales of a party rare.

Last year's fruitcake, still hard as a brick,
A mystery wrapped up in a ribbon thick.
Great Auntie Edna's bizarre dance moves,
Made everyone laugh, and nobody approves!

We pieced together the ornaments' tales,
Mixing '75 foil with '80s scales.
Who knew the holiday would keep us amused?
With blunders and laughs, no excuse to be bruised.

So here we gather with cheer and chai,
Hiding our giggles, we can't let them fly.
Shushing relatives who still wear those frowns,
This season's a riot in comfy old gowns.

Illuminated Paths of Memory

With each string of bulbs hanging just right,
We bump into memories, oh what a sight!
Grandpa's old hat, two sizes too small,
Worn with pride at the annual ball.

Uncle Fred's stories, an endless delight,
Of the time he saved Santa, and flew through the night.
Yet still we all giggle, in beings so wide,
As stories grow taller, and jokes can't abide.

The gingerbread village, completely awry,
With houses that crumble and sprinkles that fly.
We take up our spoons, and then wonder, just why,
Did we think this was better than pie by a guy?

Cousins recapture the warmth of our past,
With laughter so loud, these moments will last.
We tripped through the echoes, and dance every line,
In this merry tale, our hearts intertwine.

The Taste of Sugar and Spice

The cookies are burning, oh what a smell,
While visions of sugar plums faintly swell.
Sugar on lips, they're sticky and sweet,
Met with some laughter, our holiday treat.

A pinch of the chaos, pour in some cheer,
Add sprinkles and giggles, and trouble is near!
Flour in hair and dough on the floor,
'Tis the sweet mess we simply adore!

Pies lined up waiting, to burst with delight,
But mom shouts, "Stop! Don't eat them tonight!"
Yet one sneaky cousin, in shadows, he creeps,
Snatching a slice, while the kitchen now weeps.

Through cookies and laughter, we try to be wise,
But spice cabinet fails, with monstrous surprise.
We toast to the moments that keep us all whole,
For sugar and spice fill each joyous soul.

Sleigh Bells Ringing from Afar

Sleigh bells are ringing with whispers of cheer,
At least that's what we heard, but it's just the cat here.
She's scratching the tree, such a sight to behold,
As ornaments tumble and stories unfold.

We bundled up scarves, and ran out to play,
Until cousin Charlie claimed 'it's too cold today!'
But the snowmen appear, in all their great art,
With carrot noses that won't win the heart.

Hot cocoa awaits, with marshmallows piled,
Oh, how we all giggle, sweet sugar beguiled.
Yet someone forgot the whipped cream on top,
Now it's just cocoa, and that makes us stop.

As sleigh bells keep ringing from comfort and glee,
The joy of the season connects you and me.
So let's raise our mugs and share in the mirth,
For laughter and hugs are the best gifts on Earth.

Faded Photographs of Joy

In an album thick with cheer,
We laugh at how we used to cheer.
Grandma's hat, three sizes too large,
Made her look like a jolly sergeant!

Mismatched socks on Christmas morn,
Uncle Joe forgot to wear his shoes.
A tree that leaned a little too far,
No one could find the proper way to snooze.

Tinsel tangled like a string of fate,
While cookies vanished on a reckless plate.
Thankful for the laughs, the silly blunders,
These moments shine like festive wonders!

Oh, the gifts we wrapped with glee,
Only to find a sock or a pea.
Faded photographs on the wall,
Remind us all of our merry fall!

A Tapestry of Yuletide Memories

In a tapestry woven with love,
Lies the tale of a snowman above.
His carrot nose, it fell on the floor,
We laughed as he stared at the door!

The cat found the ribbons, oh what a sight!
Turning our gifts into a feline fight.
Mom found a hairball, yikes, what a win!
As Uncle Bob hollered, 'Let the games begin!'

Stumbling in snowdrifts, we couldn't keep straight,
Sledding down hills was a risky fate.
Each fall was a giggle, a shiver, a cheer,
These tales of mishaps, we hold dear!

Passed around stories, a toast of delight,
To the one who wore socks that were white!
With tales of mishaps brightening the night,
In this tapestry, laughter feels just right.

The Heartbeat of Frosted Joy

With mittens too big for my tiny hands,
I tried to build snowmen on shifting sands.
A mitten fell off, who knew it would roll?
Straight into the hot cocoa, like a runaway soul!

Baking cookies became a sour fate,
As the dough transformed into goo on the plate.
Sprinkles went flying, the cat in a dash,
Left icing on the floor, a sugary splash!

Granddad in his sweater, a sight to behold,
Turned too quick, got his shirt caught in the fold.
We laughed till we cried, what a merry delight,
This heartbeat of joy felt warm that night!

Memory keeps ticking, with a rhythm so sweet,
Each chuckle a lesson we will never repeat.
A heartbeat of laughter fills every space,
In the fun of the past, we find our place.

Embers of Before

In flickering lights, we see the cast,
When holiday songs were sung loud and fast.
Dad lost his voice, but he gave it a try,
The high notes fell flat, and we still laugh and sigh.

Candles tipped over, who would have thought?
Whiskers on cats caused quite the distraught.
Mom's favorite sweater caught on the spark,
Which led to giggles till well after dark!

The feast was a battle, no plates left intact,
With crumbs on the floor, a glorious fact.
The turkey ran wild, or so it seemed,
As Aunt Clara snorted, she truly redeemed!

Now we gather 'round a crackling flame,
Sharing our stories, it's always the same.
The embers of before keep us all close,
In the laughter of now, we toast to the most!

Flicker of Vintage Candles

In the corner the candles glow,
With a waxy grin, they steal the show.
Whispers of laughter, tangled in light,
Grandma's recipes still take flight.

A fruitcake sits, a fearsome sight,
It once was lovely, but now, just tight.
A slice will bounce, off the kitchen wall,
As we take turns to risk it all!

The ornaments dance on the tree,
Some are ancient, others just free.
Each one tells tales with a wink,
Of holiday cheer and bad eggnog drink!

So as we gather, let's raise a cheer,
To the vintage flair and festive gear.
With memories bright and laughter vast,
Each flicker means joy, tied to the past.

Frostbitten Pages of Time

Old albums dusted, open with care,
Frosty snapshots of moments rare.
Aunt Mildred's hat, so big and bold,
Claims the spotlight, its tales unfold.

Christmas sweaters, much too tight,
Worn with pride, oh what a sight!
Tinsel tangles and yearbook flair,
The antics caught, we're all aware.

Snowflakes swirl on the window pane,
Reminding us of childhood's reign.
Snowball fights and snowy trails,
Frostbitten giggles fill our tales.

So here we sit, with warmth and glee,
Recalling times, as wild as can be.
Though years have passed, we can't outlast,
The joy in these pages, forever cast.

Embraces Beneath Winter Stars

Under the stars, we bumble and sway,
Hugging each other, forget the fray.
Grandpa's old stories crackle with cheer,
As we all gather, so close and dear.

The hot cocoa spills, a marshmallow fight,
Laughter erupts, oh what a sight!
With snowflakes in hair, we prance around,
While puppies join in, their barks abound.

Chilly noses and cheeks a-glow,
We dance like the wind, to and fro.
Under the mistletoe, a daring smooch,
Plants and pets all giggle, what a hoot!

As winter's chill blankets the morn,
We sing our songs, tinsel is worn.
Each embrace binds us, come what may,
In warmth, we'll treasure this holiday.

Glimmers of Golden Baubles

The tree is dressed in glimmering lights,
Ornaments twinkle, what festive sights!
Crazy Uncle Joe with bells on his hat,
Wanders around, oh, where's he at?

Golden baubles swing, tempting the cat,
Who leaps with zealous, unearthly sprat.
Down they come with a joyous crash,
While laughter erupts, a hilarious splash.

Each trinket shines with a story told,
From goofy gifts to wrapping bold.
My brother dons tinsel, thinks he's a tree,
As we roll on the floor, laughing so free.

Socks as presents, a family joke,
Unused and dusty, should we invoke?
Yet in our hearts, we find the gold,
In laughter and love, treasures unfold.

The Scent of Pine and Nostalgia

In the attic, a tree from '99,
With tinsel clumped like a wild design.
Grandma's giggle, her stories grand,
And mom in a sweater, that's far from planned.

Mismatched ornaments hung with flair,
One-eyed Rudolph with a questionable stare.
Forgotten gifts under layers of dust,
Like Aunt Edna's fruitcake, it's a must!

In the corner, a box labeled 'Merry',
Filled with items outdated and hairy.
Yet every laugh brings warmth anew,
As the past slips in, like an old shoe.

So here's to the memories, mishaps and fun,
Of holidays spent, oh how we've run!
With laughter we bind all the silly and sweet,
In a joyous blend, where all hearts meet.

Lanterns of Yesteryear's Cheer

Lanterns flicker with a goofy glow,
Recalling times when we didn't know.
Dad wore a hat that was far too tall,
While trying to catch snowflakes, he slipped and did fall.

Hot cocoa spills on the carpet so bright,
Mom's secret stash? It's out of sight!
We search high and low, with whispers and glee,
Finding last year's cookies, now hard as a pea.

The carols we sing, all off the beat,
Though dad insists, he can dance on his feet.
The tall tales we spin, all wrapped in delight,
Like Grandma's eggnog that gave us a fright.

So let's raise a toast, to the blunders we find,
To the joy of the past, hilariously blind.
With lanterns aglow and laughter we cheer,
Let's cherish these moments, year after year!

Frosted Windows, Faded Wishes

Frosted windows tell a tale or two,
Of snowsuits squeezed on that one cousin Drew.
His hat was too big, his boots way too small,
He tripped in the snow and we all had a ball.

Faded wishes on old postcards lie,
A strange family photo — oh me, oh my!
Uncle bob's mustache, a sight to behold,
Looked just like a bush, oh, if truth be told!

Eggnog mischief, with sprinkles galore,
Mom said "Just sip!" but we spilled on the floor.
The cat took a leap for the jingly tree,
It's stuck in a tangle, oh woe is me!

So here's to those moments, the funny and wild,
Each year rewrites tales from the days we were styled.
Frosted windows may dim, but our laughter remains,
As we share in our stories, like old colored stains.

Chimes of Auld Lang Syne

Chimes ring out from the old clock tower,
Recalling parties at the midnight hour.
The hats we wore, such fantastical sights,
Remember when Dale danced with the lights?

We followed his lead, with arms in the air,
But tripped on the rug, oh, what a scare!
The kitchen was filled with concoctions of cheer,
And Aunt Sue's dips that became our dear fear.

The ball drops down, but wait, there's a sneeze,
The countdown is paused for a sudden 'excuse me!'
In the midst of the fun, we lost track of time,
As Grandma debates her old jingle rhyme.

So let's clink our glasses with a wink and a grin,
To the chaos and laughter, let the fun begin!
With chimes in the air and memories sound,
We dance through the night, as laughter abounds.

Wreaths of Yesterday's Joy

Once hung upon the door, so bright,
With cat's surprise, a sudden fright.
The ribbon's gone, the bow's askew,
  A Christmas tree? We had a zoo!

Those jingle bells are off the wall,
They clang and clang, just like a brawl.
Grandma's dance, oh what a sight,
She slipped, then laughed, oh what a night!

The stars we strung have lost their glow,
They wink at us, just like they know.
With sprigs of pine, we've made a mess,
  But in our hearts, our love's the best.

So raise a glass to times gone by,
With laughter loud, our spirits fly.
For joy lays hidden in each cheer,
  And every tale brings smiles near.

Vintage Ornaments and Tall Tales

A glassy bulb from '82,
Hangs precarious, who knows who?
Did Uncle Joe use it for a game?
Or was it Cousin Sue to blame?

The tinsel strewn like glittered hair,
We find it tangled everywhere.
Those stories told by fireside glow,
Got wilder each year, don't you know?

The gingerbread man lost both his feet,
He ran away using our sweet treat.
With cookies out, he's got a plan,
To chase the dog and steal the ham!

So every year we take our place,
To reenact this merry race.
With laughter rich, we toast and cheer,
For every tale that brings us near.

Comforts of Hearth and Home

The fire warms, but so does tea,
Old stories spin, come share with me.
A cat on lap, a quilt of cheer,
With every sip, the smiles appear.

Our socks are hung, but oh, what's this?
A hole so big, it's hard to miss.
Is Santa's foot not quite so small?
Or just the cat? Oh, not at all!

From kitchen smells of herbs and spice,
We've burnt our turkey, oh so nice.
Yet laughter fills the room with glee,
As we munch on leftovers, whee!

So here's to warmth, to love we share,
To messy moments, and to care.
We gather close, with hearts so warm,
In the end, it's people, the best charm.

Sweets of Pecan Pie and Remembrance

The pie is baked, or so we thought,
But where's that slice that I once sought?
Grandpa claimed he had his share,
Now suspicious, we each prepare.

A spatula flew, and who could blame?
When cousin Tim let loose his claim.
With giggles rising, our forks at hand,
It's a wrestling match—a pie demand!

We reminisce of years gone by,
The Aunt who tried her hand at pie.
With chocolate, nuts, and some great flair,
She served us crumbs, we're almost bare!

So chocolate calls, and laughter's near,
We munch on sweets and lots of cheer.
For every bite, a fond 'remember,'
With love and laughter, oh so tender.